CAROLINA PANTHERS

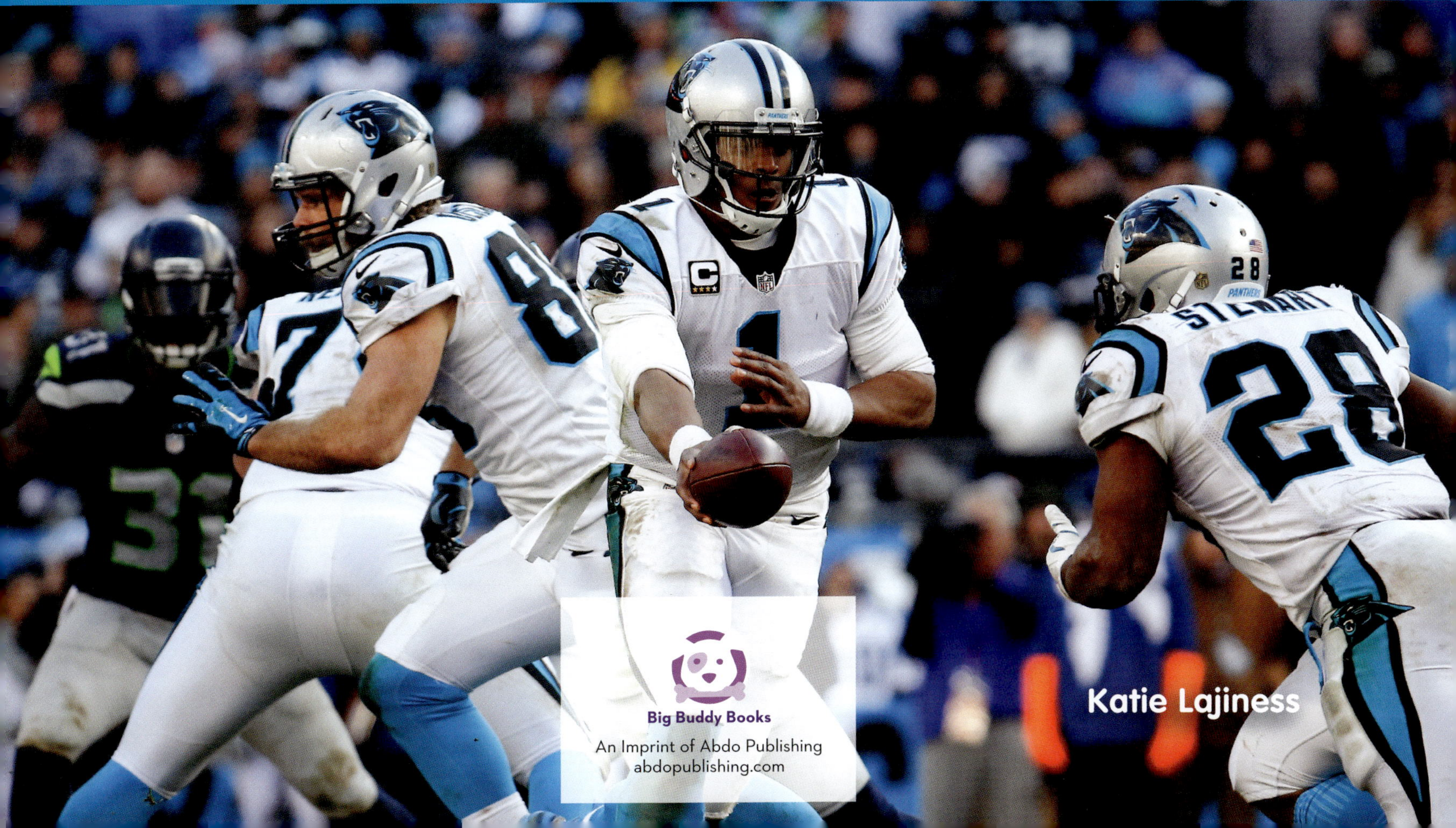

Katie Lajiness

Big Buddy Books
An Imprint of Abdo Publishing
abdopublishing.com

abdopublishing.com

Published by Abdo Publishing, a division of ABDO, PO Box 398166, Minneapolis, Minnesota 55439.

Printed in the United States of America, North Mankato, Minnesota.
092016
012017

Cover Photo: ASSOCIATED PRESS.
Interior Photos: ASSOCIATED PRESS (pp. 5, 7, 9, 10, 11, 13, 14, 15, 17, 18, 19, 20, 21, 25, 29); Cal Sport Media/Alamy Stock Photo (p. 27); Andre Jenny/Alamy Stock Photo (p. 23).

Coordinating Series Editor: Tamara L. Britton
Graphic Design: Michelle Labatt, Taylor Higgins, Jenny Christensen

Publisher's Cataloging-in-Publication Data

Names: Lajiness, Katie, author.
Title: Carolina Panthers / by Katie Lajiness.
Description: Minneapolis, MN : Abdo Publishing, 2017. | Series: NFL's greatest teams | Includes bibliographical references and index.
Identifiers: LCCN 2016944876 | ISBN 9781680785302 (lib. bdg.) | ISBN 9781680798906 (ebook)
Subjects: LCSH: Carolina Panthers (Football team)--History--Juvenile literature.
Classification: DDC 796.332--dc23
LC record available at http://lccn.loc.gov/2016944876

Contents

A Winning Team 4
League Play 6
Kicking Off 8
Highlight Reel 10
Halftime! Stat Break 14
Coaches' Corner 16
Star Players 18
Bank of America Stadium 22
Go Panthers! 24
Final Call 26
Through the Years 28
Postgame Recap 30
Glossary 31
Websites 31
Index 32

A Winning Team

The Carolina Panthers are a football team from Charlotte, North Carolina. They have played in the National Football League (NFL) for more than 20 years.

The Panthers have had good seasons and bad. But time and again, they've proven themselves. Let's see what makes the Panthers one of the NFL's greatest teams.

Blue, black, silver, and white are the team's colors.

PANTHERS

League Play

Team Standings

The NFC and the American Football Conference (AFC) make up the NFL. Each conference has a north, south, east, and west division.

The NFL got its start in 1920. Its teams have changed over the years. Today, there are 32 teams. They make up two conferences and eight divisions.

The Panthers play in the South Division of the National Football Conference (NFC). This division also includes the Atlanta Falcons, the New Orleans Saints, and the Tampa Bay Buccaneers.

The Atlanta Falcons are a major rival of the Panthers.

Kicking Off

Businessman Jerry Richardson founded the team in 1993. The Panthers began play in 1995. Like many new teams, the Panthers had a losing record their first year.

In 1996, the Panthers earned their first winning season. And, they won the NFC West Division title! The Panthers went to their first play-offs. But, they lost to the Green Bay Packers in the NFC **championship**.

In 1993, Richardson displayed the Panthers logo at a press conference.

Dom Capers was the team's first coach. He was Coach of the Year in 1996.

Highlight Reel

The Panthers struggled after their 1996 season. They continued to work hard.

Then in 2003, the team became a huge success! The Panthers finished the season with a surprising 11–5 record. They played the New England Patriots in the 2004 Super Bowl! Sadly, the Panthers lost.

Win or Go Home

NFL teams play 16 regular season games each year. The teams with the best records are part of the play-off games. Play-off winners move on to the conference championships. Then, conference winners face off in the Super Bowl!

Beyoncé sang the national anthem at the 2004 Super Bowl.

The 2004 Super Bowl was held at Reliant Stadium in Houston, Texas.

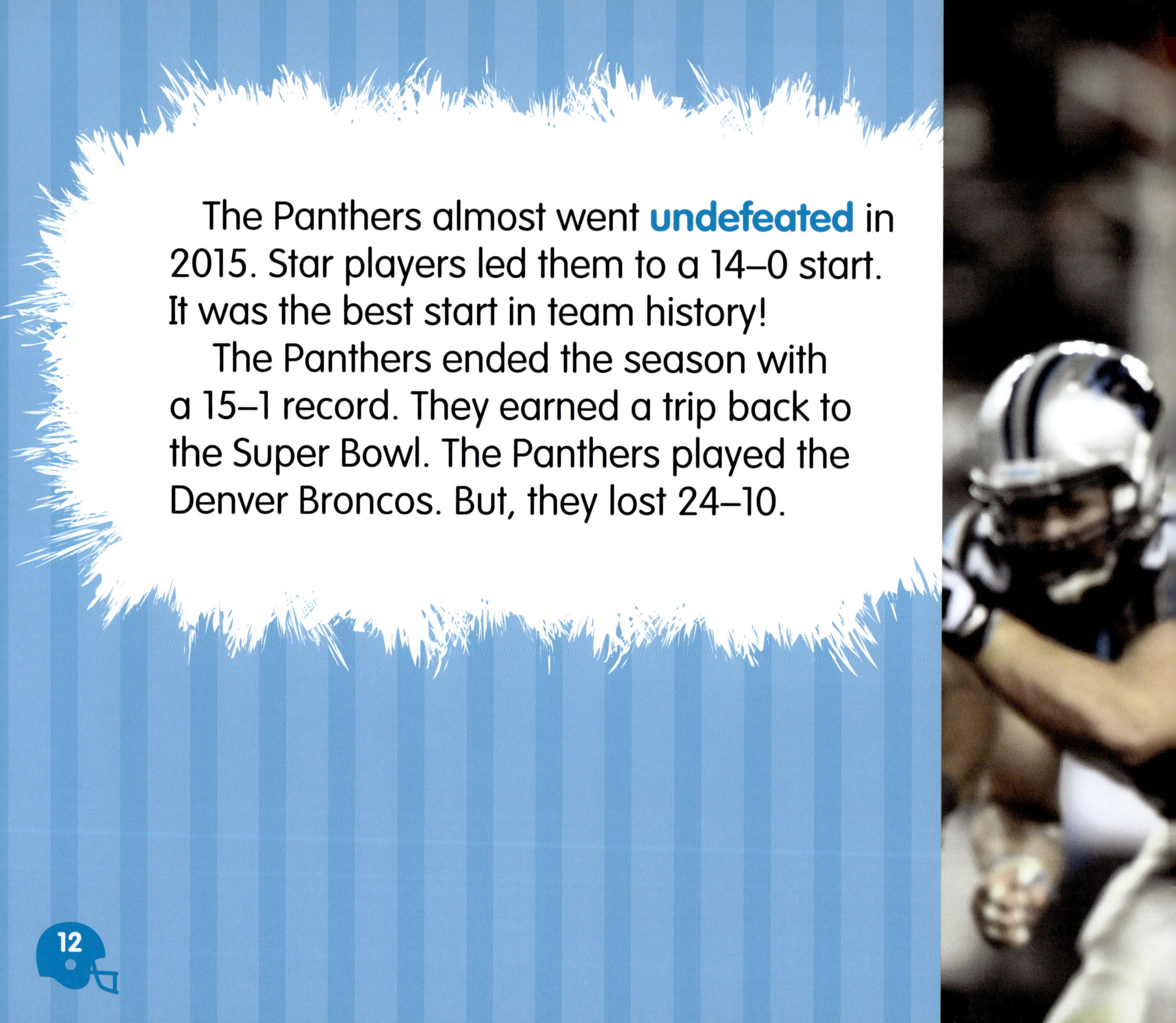

The Panthers almost went **undefeated** in 2015. Star players led them to a 14–0 start. It was the best start in team history!

The Panthers ended the season with a 15–1 record. They earned a trip back to the Super Bowl. The Panthers played the Denver Broncos. But, they lost 24–10.

In 2015, Cam Newton was named NFL Most Valuable Player (MVP).

Halftime! Stat Break

Team Records

RUSHING YARDS
Career: DeAngelo Williams, 6,846 yards (2006–2014)
Single Season: DeAngelo Williams, 1,515 yards (2008)

PASSING YARDS
Career: Jake Delhomme, 19,258 yards (2003–2009)
Single Season: Steve Beuerlein, 4,436 yards (1999)

RECEPTIONS
Career: Steve Smith, 836 receptions (2001–2013)
Single Season: Steve Smith, 103 receptions (2005)

ALL-TIME LEADING SCORER
John Kasay, 1,482 points (1995–2010)

Famous Coaches

Dom Capers (1995–1998)
John Fox (2002–2010)

Championships

SUPER BOWL APPEARANCES:
2004, 2016

SUPER BOWL WINS:
None

Pro Football Hall of Famers & Their Years with the Panthers

None

Fan Fun

STADIUM: Bank of America Stadium
LOCATION: Charlotte, North Carolina
MASCOT: Sir Purr
TEAM SONG: "Stand and Cheer"

Coaches' Corner

John Fox became the head coach of the Panthers in 2002. He coached the team for nine seasons. Under his leadership, the team won the most games in Panthers history. And, the Panthers appeared in two NFC **championships** and one Super Bowl!

Ron Rivera joined the Panthers in 2011. He led the team to three straight divisional titles. And, the Panthers played in the Super Bowl. Rivera was named NFL Coach of the Year in 2013 and 2015.

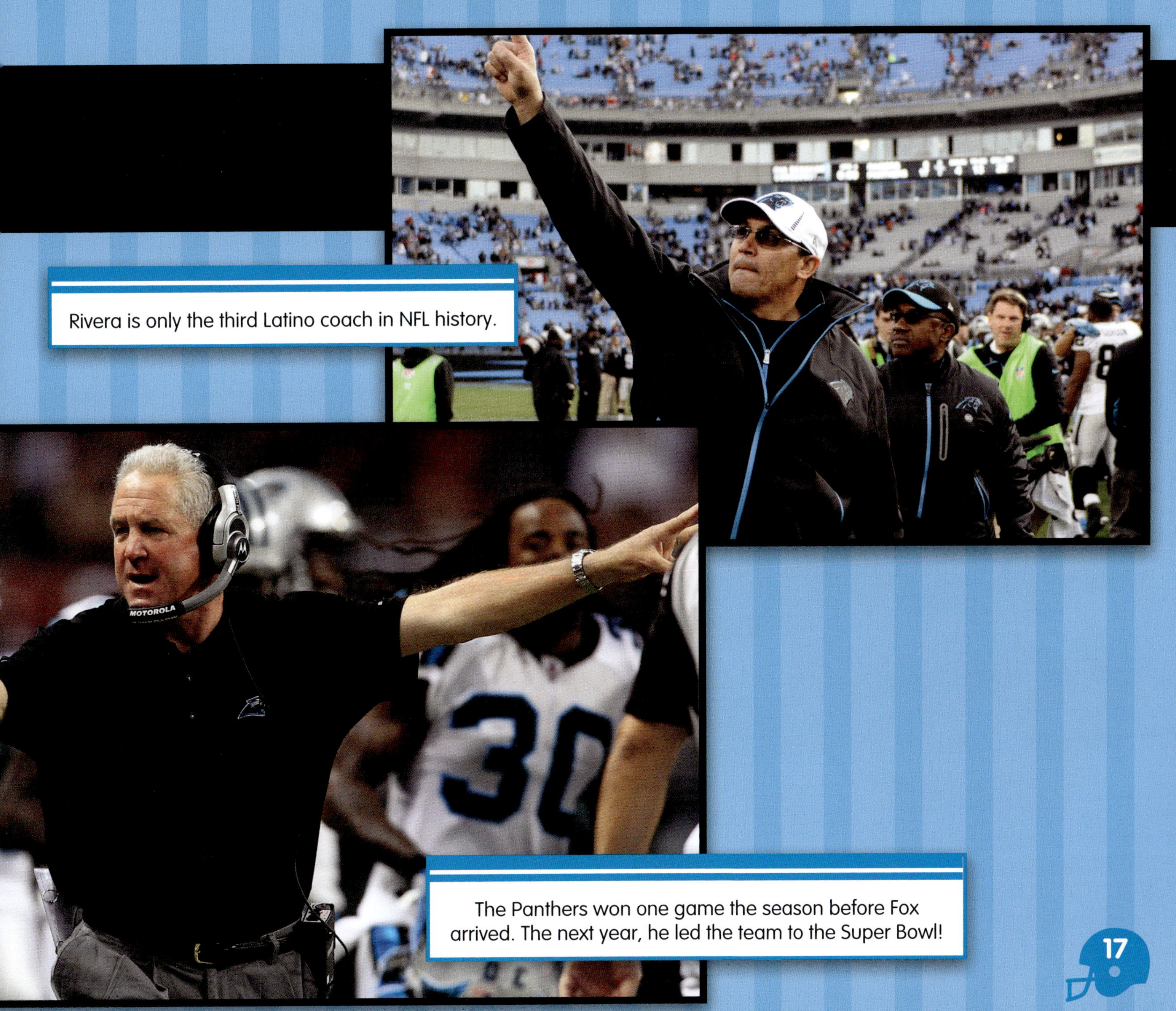

Rivera is only the third Latino coach in NFL history.

The Panthers won one game the season before Fox arrived. The next year, he led the team to the Super Bowl!

Star Players

Sam Mills LINEBACKER (1995–1997)

Sam Mills joined the Panthers in 1995. He was chosen to play in five Pro Bowls. This is the NFL's all-star game. Mills was the only player to start every game during the team's first three seasons. In 1998, the Panthers named Mills to their Hall of Honor.

John Kasay PLACEKICKER (1995–2010)

John Kasay joined the Panthers during their first season. In 1996, he kicked 37 field goals. That was an NFL record at the time. Three years later, he made his 400th field goal. He holds almost every Panthers kicking record. And, he is the team's all-time points leader.

Steve Smith WIDE RECEIVER (2001–2013)

During the 2003 NFC Division play-offs, Smith caught a 69-yard touchdown pass. This helped the team beat the Los Angeles Rams 29–23. Smith had his best season in 2005. He led the league in receiving yards, receptions, and touchdowns.

Thomas Davis LINEBACKER (2005–)

Thomas Davis was selected in the first round of the 2005 **draft**. Davis is known as a tough player. He had surgery on the same knee three times. In 2014, Davis was honored with an **award** for his community work.

Cam Newton QUARTERBACK (2011–)

Cam Newton was the number one draft pick in 2011. He was an instant star player! Newton became the first quarterback to throw for 400 yards in his first game. He also set NFL records for passing and rushing yards that season. Newton was named NFL **Rookie** of the Year.

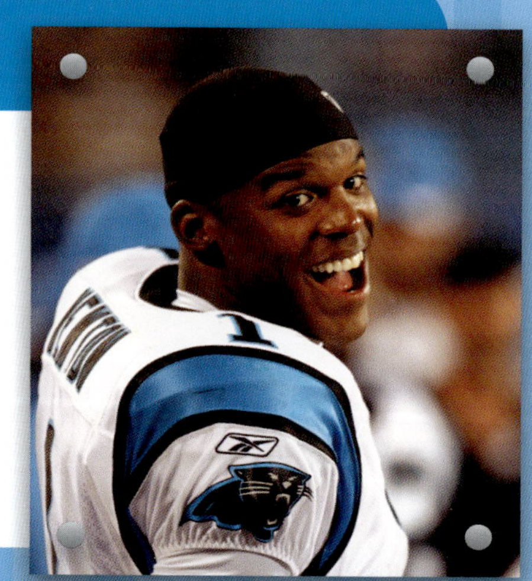

Greg Olsen TIGHT END (2011–)

In 2011, Greg Olsen joined the Panthers. During his first season, he made five touchdowns. In 2015, Olsen finished the regular season with 77 receptions for 1,104 yards and seven touchdowns. He holds the team records for receiving yards and receptions for a tight end.

Luke Kuechly LINEBACKER (2012–)

In 2012, Luke Kuechly had an awesome start to his NFL **career**! He was named Defensive **Rookie** of the Year that season. The next year, Kuechly became the youngest player to win the Defensive Player of the Year **award**. He was chosen to play in three Pro Bowls.

Bank Of America Stadium

The Panthers play home games at Bank of America Stadium. It is in Charlotte. The stadium opened in 1996. It can hold more than 75,000 people.

Six bronze panthers border the stadium's three main entrances. The statues are the largest ever built in the United States.

Go Panthers!

Thousands of fans flock to Bank of America Stadium to see the Panthers play home games. In 1995, Sir Purr became the team's **mascot**. He wears a jersey with the number 00. Sir Purr helps fans cheer on the team.

Sir Purr works with NFL Play 60. This group teaches kids to move their bodies for better health.

SIR PURR
Play 60

Final Call

The Panthers have a long, rich history. They played in Super Bowls 2004 and 2016.

Even during losing seasons, true fans have stuck by them. Many believe the Panthers will remain one of the greatest teams in the NFL.

The Panthers celebrate a 2016 win against their rivals, the Tampa Bay Buccaneers.

Through the Years

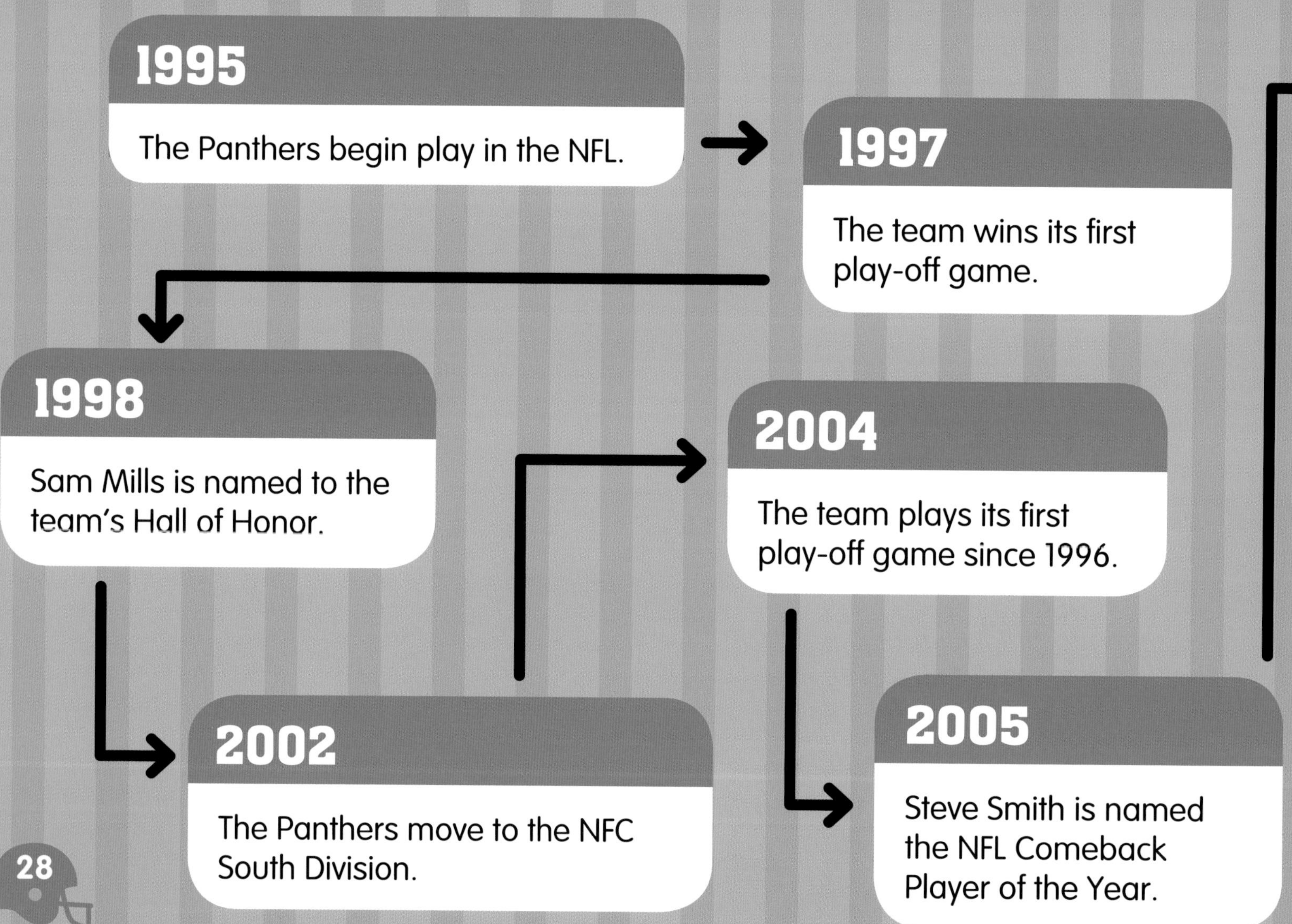

2011

The Panthers pick Cam Newton first in the NFL **draft**.

2012

A new team **logo** is created for the team.

2015

The team has its best season with a 15-1 record.

2016

The Panthers play the Denver Broncos in the Super Bowl.

Postgame Recap

1. Who is the team's mascot?
   A. Pink Panther **B**. Sir Purr **C**. Jaxon de Ville

2. Where do the Panthers play home games?
   A. EverBank Field
   B. U.S. Bank Stadium
   C. Bank of America Stadium

3. What year did the Panthers begin play?
   A. 1995
   B. 1996
   C. 1997

4. Which coach led the Panthers to their most wins in team history?
   A. John Fox
   B. Ron Rivera
   C. Mike Wazowski

1. B. 2. C. 3. A. 4. A.

Glossary

award something that is given in recognition of good work or a good act.

career a period of time spent in a certain job.

championship a game, a match, or a race held to find a first-place winner.

draft a system for professional sports teams to choose new players.

logo a symbol that is used to identify a company and that appears on its products.

mascot something to bring good luck and help cheer on a team.

rookie a first-year player in a professional sport.

undefeated not having any losses.

Websites

To learn more about the NFL's Greatest Teams, visit **booklinks.abdopublishing.com**. These links are routinely monitored and updated to provide the most current information available.

Index

American Football Conference **6**
Atlanta Falcons **6, 7**
Bank of America Stadium **15, 22, 23, 24**
Beyoncé **10**
Capers, Dom **9, 14**
Davis, Thomas **20**
Denver Broncos **12, 29**
fans **24, 26**
Fox, John **14, 16, 17**
Green Bay Packers **8**
Kasay, John **14, 19**
Kuechly, Luke **21**
Los Angeles Rams **19**
mascot **15, 24**
Mills, Sam **18, 28**
National Football Conference **6, 8, 16, 19, 28**
National Football League **4, 6, 10, 13, 16, 17, 19, 20, 21, 24, 26, 28, 29**
New England Patriots **10**
New Orleans Saints **6**
Newton, Cam **13, 20, 29**
North Carolina **4, 15, 22**
Olsen, Greg **21**
play-offs **8, 10, 19, 28**
Pro Bowl **18, 21**
Pro Football Hall of Fame **15**
Reliant Stadium **11**
Richardson, Jerry **8, 9**
Rivera, Ron **16, 17**
Smith, Steve **14, 19, 28**
South Division **6, 16, 28**
Super Bowl **10, 11, 12, 14, 16, 17, 26, 29**
Tamp Bay Buccaneers **6, 27**
Texas **11**
United States **23**